Discovering the Magic of Math ©

An Upper Elementary and Junior High Teaching Manual

By
Walt Belsky
&
Greg Laufer

Illustrated by Teresa Belsky

Foreword by Nancy L. Johnson

Prism Educational
Services

Sparta, Illinois

Prism Educational Services

Sparta, Illinois

Prism Educational Services
275 Prairie Lane
Sparta, Illinois 62286

Printed in the United States of America

ISBN: 0-9653980-0-5

10 9 8 7 6 5 4 3 2

Discovering the Magic of Math

Table of Contents

Foreword..5

Introduction..6

Conjuring a Number Between 1 and 1000........................9

Instant Addition...15

Rapid Multiplication...21

Lightning Addition...31

The Impossible Paper..45

The Jumping Paper Clips..51

The String Escape...59

The Sequential Four of a Kind......................................67

Social Security Number Test...73

Writing Activities.........................14, 20, 30, 93, 94, 95

Foreword
By
Nancy L. Johnson

Discovering the Magic of Math
By
Walt Belsky and Greg Laufer

When I first met Greg Laufer I knew he was someone special. He reminded me of my former gifted students. Bright, idealistic, talented, focused---radiating potential. And even though he was young, still in the early stages of his career, he possessed a mature, sincere desire to improve education. This genuine attitude to help teachers and their students came shining through his highly motivational presentations.

Like some mythical Pied Piper, I saw Greg lead his audience into discovering the magic of math. Hmmm...sounds like a good book title! When teachers started asking (at times begging!) for more ideas, Greg joined forces with his business partner, Walt Belsky, to produce this practical guide for using magic as a motivational tool to teach math.

- *As you thumb through this book you will find lots of **SURPRISES!***

- *The activities are hands-on--- a true application of mathematical concepts.*

- *Students are challenged to not only use math skills, but also to think mathematically.*

- *The lessons are saturated with cross-content writing activities.*

- *The mathematics is grounded in topological **problem solving**.*

Take a "piece of Greg" home with you . Have fun along with your students in rediscovering the joy of math.

You've come a long way, Greg. Congratulations!

Nancy L. Johnson, President
Pieces of Learning
Creative Learning Consultants, Inc.

Introduction
by
Walter F. Belsky

<u>Discovering the Magic of Math</u> has taken three years of writing and thirty years of preparation!

My first teaching opportunity was in an inner city school. I quickly discovered that quality hands-on activities would normally produce great results. Positive academic progress and improved behavior patterns developed whenever I gained the students' interest. Usually, success would be guaranteed by using lots of manipulatives. This was true in all areas of the curriculum.

In my first teaching year a little boy named Juan was placed in my class. Juan had just moved to the city from Puerto Rico. He spoke no English....I spoke no Spanish. I felt that I was in for a challenging year.

We worked together for the school year. Juan was exposed to a variety of learning styles. I quickly discovered that he would retain lots of information when he was taught using a variety of hands-on activities. No language was necessary.

His greatest advances were in mathematics. In this area, Juan was consistently at the top of the class. The school psychologist, the language teacher, and my administrators were inquisitive and excited about his success. Juan's academic achievement was the discussion topic at several meetings.

My teaching strategies were investigated. All agreed that Juan could learn mathematics concepts without verbalization. And, he had learned through numerous hands-on exercises.

I had experienced a great lesson early in my career; high quality learning takes place when the teacher uses a variety of teaching styles. For Juan, it was the hands-on activities. Other students may be successful with traditional methods.

My experiences with Juan led me to be a collector, a collector of manipulatives. Over the years I have gathered some really neat hands-on activities. An effort has been made to always provide some planned activity combined with manipulatives to explain a particular concept.

This is especially true when I teach mathematics. My need to make mathematics highly visible led to the idea that many principles could be explained through magic. Magic seems to grasp a child's attention; at the same time the student wonders how and why a particular effect takes place. And, it's great for brainstorming.

Greg Laufer is a family friend and a co-author of <u>Discovering the Magic of Math</u>. Together we have developed a program that uses magic to help explain mathematics. We are in our fourth year of developing workshops for students, parents, and educators.

Our business, Prism Educational Services, is constantly receiving favorable comments. Workshop participants are often amazed when we demonstrate a mathematical principle and its application using magic.

Care is taken to inform everyone that there is no such thing as magic. The honest explanation is that Greg or I know something about geometry, multiplication, or addition that is not yet known by the workshop participants. After several hours of intensive activities students, teachers, or parents leave a workshop with a renewed interest into the complexities of the mathematical sciences.

This text has been prepared for teachers at all grade levels. It is a useful tool that can be used to help educators grasp a child's attention. Hopefully, fellow educators will study the materials; then some of the information can be used to put lots of motivational magic into the classroom.

Note pages are located throughout the text. Use them whenever there are questions or ideas you may want to save.

Notes

Conjuring a Number Between 1 and 1000?

Select a correct answer from a thousand possibilities.

The Effect

The teacher turns his back to the blackboard. A student is asked to write a three-digit number, all digits being different. Next, that number is reversed and recorded on the board. Instruct the class to observe the two numbers, maybe 138 and 831. Have them place a check mark in front of the number with the greatest value.

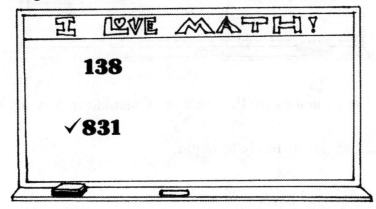

On a separate part of the board, rewrite the biggest number. Below it place the smaller number. Put in a subtraction sign and have a horizontal line drawn.

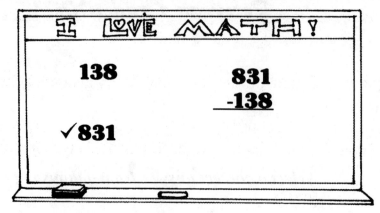

Since Conjuring a Number is an exercise in following directions, repeat the directions a second time.

Select a student with a strong understanding of borrowing. Instruct the student to complete the calculation.

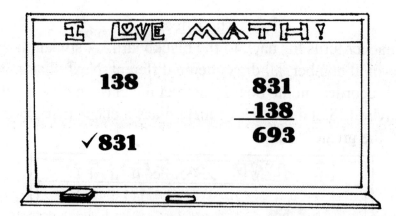

Allow a few minutes for the solution. Calculators may also be used.

The exciting part is ready to begin.

Ask the class how many numbers there are from one to a thousand. You might explain there are about 1000.

State that even though you have strong mathematical abilities, it is not possible to calculate this answer without some help from the students. Ask for someone to give the last digit of the answer.

When the final digit is given, you immediately announce the answer to the subtraction problem.

Imagine that! You still have your back turned away from the board!

Objectives

At the conclusion of Conjuring Numbers, the students will have learned the following:

- There will be an improvement of the skills needed in borrowing.

- The concept of place value will be reinforced.

- Students' listening skills will be improved by following verbal directions.

- There will be an understanding that numbers follow a distinct pattern. Predictions can be made based on these patterns.

The Method

Whenever a three-digit number, all digits being different, is reversed and subtracted, the answer will always have a nine as the center number. The first and last digits also add up to nine. The only possible answers for these types of problems are:

099	**594**
198	**693**
297	**792**
396	**891**
495	**990**

If the class responds that you gave an incorrect answer, you might reply that maybe there has been some minor miscalculation in their subtraction. Have them double check the borrowing.

The students will gain additional insight when they recognize the number patterns in the routine.

1) All of the numbers are multiples of 9 and 99.

2) The hundreds place value is always ascending.

3) The ones place value is always descending.

4) When added together, the ones digit and the hundreds digit equal the tens digit.

5) When each digit is added horizontally, the sum is 18.

Conclusion

Conjuring Numbers is an exciting math manipulative. It can be adapted for use in multiple grade levels. Younger students are fascinated by the thought of their teacher selecting a number from 1000 choices. Older children may want to brainstorm and find additional uses and applications for this magic effect.

Notes

You have been selected to design the cover for a book on math magic. Draw the cover. Markers, crayons, and colorded pencils may be used.

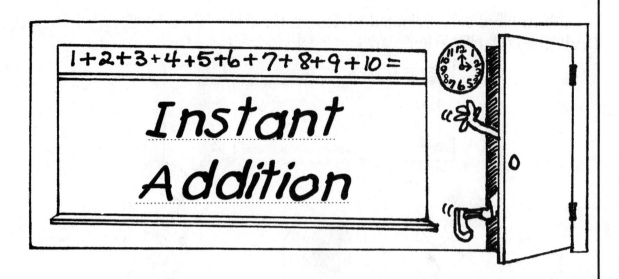

Instant Addition. . . . Look at a column of numbers. . . . Instantly announce a sum.

The Effect

The teacher explains that a student has learned the art of instant addition. The student can look at a column of three-digit numbers and immediately announce a sum.

Naturally, all want to see a performance.

The student with this "mystical" ability is asked to leave the room, and take a friend with them.

A three-digit number is supplied by a student and written on the board. The teacher offers a second number placed below the first. A third number is added by a different student, followed by another from the teacher. Finally, another student is asked to write a final three-digit number.

Explain that the last number was supplied by a student, not the teacher; any number could have been selected.

The volunteer is told to enter the room and observe the column of numbers. A sum is quickly announced.

Calculators can now be used to check the answer. Surprisingly, the student has accurately announced the sum for the randomly selected numbers.

Objectives

Students will achieve the following results through the use of Rapid Addition:

- There will be an increased awareness of the significance of place value.

- Students will realize the importance of carrying and its domino effect.

- Students will have a valuable experience using a calculator.

- The class will become more aware of the uses of patterning and sequencing in predicting an outcome.

The Student's Role

Instant Addition is an exercise that can be used with a volunteer. Explain the three steps necessary to solving the Instant Addition routine.

1) Only the very last number, the fifth in the column, is necessary to answer the problem. Focus on this number.

2) Mentally, place a 2 in front of the fifth row of digits. Suppose 378 were in this position. Simply put a 2 in front; the new number would be 2,378.

3) Decrease the new number by 2, or 2,378 minus 2 equals 2,376. The answer would be 2,376

Student Summation

Step 1) Look at the fifth number in the column. Place a two in front. Subtract two from the last digit.

Step 2) The two middle digits remain unchanged.

Examples

Step 1   *Step 2*
476 changes into 2,476; then 2,474

589 changes into 2,589; then 2,587

171 changes into 2,171; then 2,169

Mathematical development

The teacher, not the student, determines the final summation. The student has some information not understood by the class. After the initial three-digit number has been volunteered by a student, the teacher adds his/her number. The teacher simply makes the sum of the first two numbers equal to 999. Example: The student writes 812. The teacher writes 187.

$$
\begin{array}{r}
\mathbf{812} \\
+\ \mathbf{187} \\
\hline
\mathbf{999}
\end{array}
\quad
\begin{array}{l}
\textit{Student Number} \\
\textit{Teacher Number} \\
\
\end{array}
$$

The second set of numbers can now be written:

$$
\begin{array}{r}
\mathbf{106} \\
+\ \mathbf{803} \\
\hline
\mathbf{999}
\end{array}
\quad
\begin{array}{l}
\textit{Student Number} \\
\textit{Teacher Number} \\
\
\end{array}
$$

Look at an example as it would appear in the classroom.

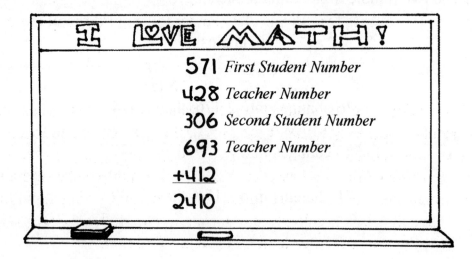

I LOVE MATH!

571 *First Student Number*
428 *Teacher Number*
306 *Second Student Number*
693 *Teacher Number*
+412
2410

This particular type of problem is perfect for magical manipulation. The first two numbers are added to equal 999; the second group also has the 999 sum. And, added together, they equal 1998. Any three-digit number added to 1998 will equal to a number of 2,000 plus.

Remember, for the answer, the student who assisted the teacher was instructed to place a 2 in front of the fifth three-digit number. Then he/she subtracted two from that number.

Occasionally, a zero or a one will be written in the units place.

Example: 7 4 0 or 351

The 0 in 740 and the 1 in 351 are low numbers. If 740 or 351 were used, the sequencing of numbers in the tens place value would change. **The problem can still be solved by following the same steps. Yet, it might present a problem for students not fully acquainted with place value.**

Since you direct the number flow in this magical effect, it would be wise to ask the student supplying the last number to select one with a digit higher than a 0 or 1 in the units place. Students are willing to change their choice since they assume the higher the number the more difficult the answer.

Conclusion

Rapid addition gives students a valuable tool to use in investigating number theory, especially the multiple uses of the numbers 9 and 999.

Once Instant Addition has been mastered the multiple classroom uses may be investigated. Use it as a reward. Teach it when learning about place value; or, have the class break into groups and let the students develop their own magic using the principles learned in Rapid Addition.

You know a fellow student is visually impaired. There is going to be a math magic show. What steps would you take beforehand to insure this student realized the full effect of each routine?

_____

_____

_____

_____

_____

_____

_____

_____

"Abracadabra"

WOW!

YEA!!!

Cool!

Rapid Multiplication

The teacher picks a correct number from a million choices.

<u>The Effect</u>

A chalk or marlite board is divided into two columns, labeled A and B. A volunteer is asked to think of a three-digit number. Then write this number in column A and again in column B.

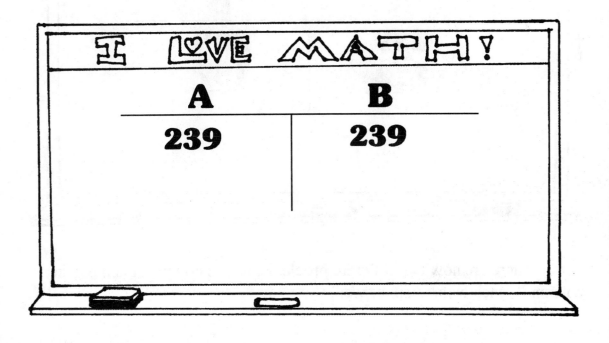

The teacher concentrates on both numbers. After a few moments, something is written down. The teacher announces, "I've made a prediction and it's written on this sheet of paper. I'm going to seal it in this envelope. Would someone please hold my prediction?"

The prediction is placed in an envelope. It is sealed and given to a student.

Someone then writes a second three-digit number below the first in column A. A multiplication sign is placed in front of the second number and a straight line drawn.

Next, the teacher supplies a number and writes it below the first in column B. The multiplication sign and horizontal line are drawn in the proper position.

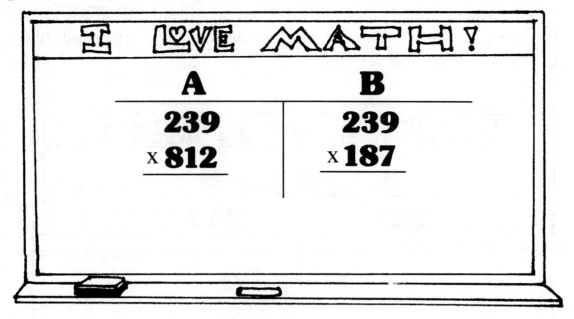

There are now two different problems, one in column A and one in column B, each without an answer.

Distribute four to six calculators. Have the students find the products of A and B. Write the answers on the board. Make sure the students' answers agree.

The person holding the envelope is asked to open it to see if the numbers on the board match the prediction.

This being done, the reply is, "No!"

The teacher comments, "There must be some sort of mistake. It always worked in the past."

The teacher has a baffled facial expression. Finally, there is a verbal response. "Oh! Try this....... Add the products in columns A and B together."

The numbers are added. The new sum is recorded on the board.

I LOVE MATH!

A	B
239	239
x 812	x 187
194,068 ⟵----- + -----⟶ 44,693	
= 238,761	

Ask the person holding the prediction to say the number on the sheet of paper; it may also be shown to the class.

The numbers match!

Explain that you had mentally multiplied columns A and B but had failed to state the products would be added to arrive at a correct prediction.

Have your students think about the number of possibilities you had to choose from. The volunteer had a free choice of all three-digit numbers with all the digits being different. This makes the number range from 102 to 987. That's a lot of numbers!

Since you multiplied two three-digit numbers together, consider the number of combinations. Now is a good time to discuss what happens when two three-digit numbers are multiplied together. Often a six-digit answer is the result. There is the possibility of a five-digit answer. Since most students enjoy using large numbers, the product will most likely contain six-digits.

Have the students look at the range of numbers in a five or six-digit product. Begin at 10,000 and end at 999,999. If you estimate the amount of numbers in the range, it is about ten thousand less then one million. One million would be a good approximation. Out of those million numbers you predicted the answer.

The Objectives

At the conclusion of Rapid Multiplication, the students will have learned the following:

- Large numbers can be constructed from a series of smaller numbers.

- The understanding of algebraic equations can sometimes be simplified by explaining them in terms of their arithmetical applications.

- Students will be more proficient and willing to use the calculator to explore and answer abstract number applications.

- The meaning of the mathematical terms "product" and "sum" will be understood through their use in Rapid Multiplication.

- The uses and applications of the distributive property of addition will be enhanced.

Preparation

Rapid Multiplication requires minimal preparation time. Be sure to have calculators. Students may use their own or borrow from a classroom set. Have an envelope and a piece of paper.

Mathematics Background

The paradox of Rapid Multiplication is no multiplication is ever needed to make the prediction.

With only one number, a prediction can be made. Based solely on the first number, the teacher automatically deduces an accurate answer. This is how it works.

Phase 1: The Six-Digit Prediction

The prediction requires two steps.

Step one is to perform a very simple mathematical calculation. The student first writes the same three-digit number in columns A and B. After viewing the first number, the teacher writes a number that is one less than the student's on the piece of paper. If the student had supplied the number 376, the teacher would have written 375; or, if the first number were 520 then 519 would be written. Mathematically, the teacher's number is in the thousands place and will be read as 375,000 and 519,000. There will be more about reading the first three digits later in the chapter.

Try these:

Student's Number	Teacher's Number
216	215
394	(A)_____
518	(B)_____
107	(C)_____

Answers: A = 393   B = 517   C = 106

Step two, predicting the second three-digit number is somewhat more challenging, but relatively easy.

In the example in the last paragraph, 376 was changed into 375 and recorded by the teacher. The 375 is now used to determine the teacher's second three-digit number.

To solve the second part of the prediction, subtract the teacher's first number from 999, or 999-375=624

$$\begin{array}{r} 999 \\ -375 \\ \hline 624 \end{array}$$

The 624 is the second three-digit number.

At first it might seem awkward to do the mental calculation in front of a room full of students; it is really very easy.

There is another method of computing the answer. Instead of subtracting the three-digit numbers, think of the problem as three one-digit problems; 9-5=4, 9-7=2, 9-3=6. There's no borrowing. As long as the place values are kept in the correct sequence, it will work every time. See Example 1.

After a few minutes of practice you'll become comfortable enough to want to perform Rapid Multiplication before your students.

Example 1

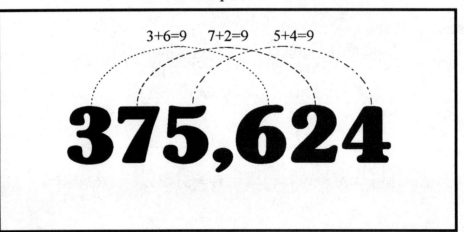

Try these:

Student's First Three-Digit Number	Teacher's First Three-Digit Number	Teacher's Second Three-Digit Number	Six-Digit Prediction
219	218,	781	218,781
583	582,	417	(A)_____
947	(B)___ ,	053	(C)_____
459	(D)___ ,	(E)____	(F)_____

Answers: A) 582,417; B) 946; C) 946,053; D) 458; E) 541; F) 458,541

Now we're going to learn how the teacher knows what to write in column B.

Phase 2: Setting Up the Problem

How does the teacher know which number to write in column B? This is an integral part of the prediction; and, care must be taken.

Fortunately the last step is easy to determine. The teacher simply uses the student's <u>second number</u> in column A as a guideline. This number is matched with an unknown quantity to equal 999.

Assume the second student volunteered 814. The teacher would have written 185 as the second number in column B, since 814 + 185 = 999!

* Remember to use the digit-by-digit principle from Example 1.

Try these:

	Student's Number (Second Number in Column A)		Teacher's Written Response	
236	+	763	= 999	
319	+	680	= 999	
512	+	A	= 999	
308	+	B	= 999	
910	+	C	= 999	

A)_____   B)_____   C)_____

Practice

1) 859   859
    x 614   x __E__

    Prediction = ___D___

2) 325   325
    x 148   x __G__

    Prediction = ___F___

3) 473   473
    x 842   x __I__

    Prediction = ___H___

4) 583   583
    x 214   x __K__

    Prediction = ___J___

Answers: A = 487   B = 691   C = 89
    1) D: 858,141 E: 385; 2) F: 324,675 G: 851;
    3) H: 472,527 I: 157; 4) J: 582,417 K:785

Follow these steps to become proficient in **Rapid Multiplication.**

1) After the first number is given, perhaps 376, the teacher reduces it by 1, to obtain 375.

2) Write the 375 on the sheet of paper.

3) Obtain the second three digits by mentally subtracting the teacher's first number, 375 from 999.

$$\begin{array}{r} 999 \\ -375 \\ \hline 624 \end{array}$$

Write 624 after 375. The prediction is complete .....3 7 5, 6 2 4. It is read three hundred seventy-five thousand, six hundred twenty-four.

4) A student writes a second three digit number in column A.

5) The teacher uses the same method explained in step 3. Mentally, subtract the student's second number from 999. Write this number on the board under 376 in column B.

6) Calculate the answers.

7) Open the prediction. Accept the fact........... The teacher is really a magician!

Conclusion

Rapid Multiplication is a great way to demonstrate how to combine the unusual characteristics of 999 with the distributive property of addition. The teacher has a very useful tool to motivate students.

Practice the steps several times before a class performance. Teach it to your students. They will gain enormous pride and satisfaction when they learn to demonstrate their multiplication skills. Once all the steps are mastered, students might search for additional uses and applications for the magical number 999.

The complexities of Rapid Multiplication can be challenging. Your effort will pay big dividends. Students will have pride and satisfaction once they understand number prediction.

Perform a magic routine for someone in your family. Describe their reaction to your magic abilities.

LIGHTNING ADDITION

Instant Addition......Look at a column of numbers.....Announce the sum!

The Effect

The mathemagician (you) tells the students that you can add faster than a calculator, even big three-digit numbers. A stack of numbered cards is shown; all have four digits arranged in vertical columns.

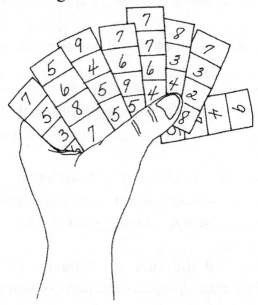

A class volunteer is selected and handed the cards. Instructions are given to shuffle the stack and select three cards. They are to be placed side by side on the Lighting Worksheet under columns A, B, and C (See Example A).

Allow the volunteer time to select the cards and place them on the worksheet. Look to make sure the directions are understood. If not, show the student where to place the cards.

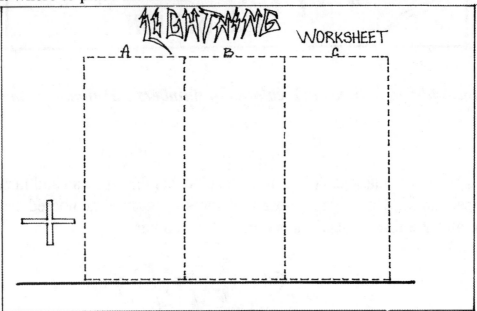

Example A

Next, the three original cards are placed back in the pile. Reshuffle. Choose three new cards. This time the teacher will not view the cards on the Lightning Worksheet.

Distribute several calculators to the students.

Restate that one of your specialties is lightning addition. Explain that it is possible to calculate the sum of three numbers more quickly than they, even while using a calculator.

Let the students with the calculators stand in full view of the Lightning Worksheet. They are to begin to add the numbers on the count of three.

Count..... One.....Two.....Three...

The students start adding. The mathemagician casually looks at the cards and immediately writes or calls out the sum of the number cards.

The effect may be repeated a second time. There will always be a different sum. Please note: To maintain the effectiveness of all math magic, it is recommended they not be repeated more than once or twice.

Step by Step Review

1) Select a volunteer.
2) Display the number cards. Choose three.
3) Demonstrate the card placement. Help, if needed.
4) Announce you are going to add faster than a calculator.
5) Distribute the calculators.
6) Arrange students with the calculators in full view of the worksheet.
7) Return the original cards to the deck. Shuffle. A student selects three and place them on the Lightning Worksheet.
8) Begin the count one.......two........three.
9) Add the numbers using the calculators.
10) Walk to the worksheet. Look at the cards and announce the sum.

Objectives

At the conclusion of Lighting Addition, the following objectives will be achieved:

- Students will investigate addition fact theory.

- The concept for sum and place value will be developed.

- The students will use calculators to solve a mathematical equation.

- The class will gain insight into problem solving and number analysis.

- The students will continue to develop fine motor skills.

- Hand-eye coordination will be improved.

The Explanation

Lightning Addition uses two mathematical manipulations. The first is all numbers in the vertical columns are arranged in a pattern. The pattern uses the third-digit from the top of the column to identify the location of a <u>key or prepared number.</u> Imagine the card in Example 2 had been selected.

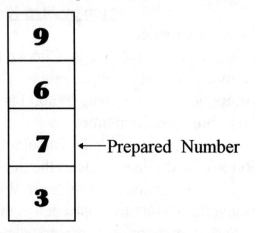

Example 2

Note: The Prepared Number need not be in the third location in the column. But, its placement must be consistent throughout the routine.

Notice the location of the seven, the third spot in the column. Therefore, seven is the key or Prepared Number. The next step is simple. Subtract two from the Prepared Number. Write the answer in the ones place.

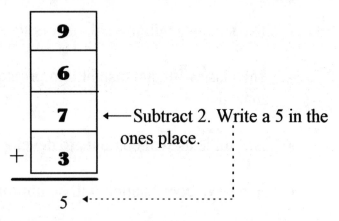

In the next five problems, what digit would you write in the ones place?

$$
\begin{array}{l}
1) \ 7 \\
 5 \\
 3 \leftarrow \text{Prepared Number, subtract 2} \\
 \underline{+6} \\
 1 \leftarrow \text{Answer}
\end{array}
$$

2) 5	3) 8	4) 3	5) 7
6	4	7	3
8	5	9	2
+7	+ 6	+ 8	+ 8

Answers: 2) 6   3) 3   4) 7   5) 0

The second manipulation uses a magic technique called a force. Magicians sometimes use a force to help prove a prediction. The manipulation or force in Lightning Addition is all the individual cards are arranged to have a sum in the twenties. A two will always be written in the tens column.

Let's re-examine problems 1 to 5. Note the digits in the units place.

1) 7	2) 5	3) 8	4) 3	5) 7
5	6	4	7	3
3	8	5	9	2
+ 6	+ 7	+ 6	+ 8	+ 8
1	6	3	7	0

Place a 2 in the tens place. The answers are 21, 26, 23, 27, and 20.

Write the sums for the next five problems. Remember to use the two manipulations.

6	7	8	9	5
4	5	7	4	9
2	3	4	5	6
+ 8	+ 6	+ 3	+ 5	+ 4

Finding the sum for multiple cards is simple. Card X (See below) has a sum of 26. Card Y's sum is 25.

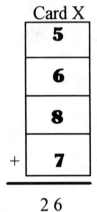

When the cards are placed side by side their sum is 2 8 5.

5	9
6	3
8	7
+ 7	6

2   8   5

The first rule still applies. Find the Prepared Number. Subtract 2. Write the answer in the units place.

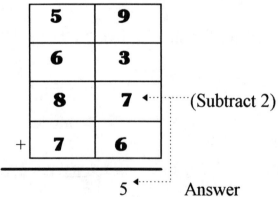

In multi-column addition problems the second rule changes. When there are two or more numbers, write the numbers that are immediately to the left of the Prepared Number.

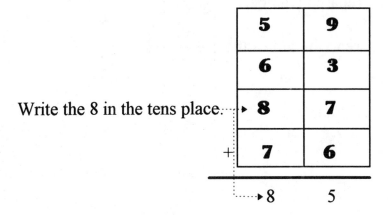

Write the 8 in the tens place.

Next, place a 2 in the left hand column.

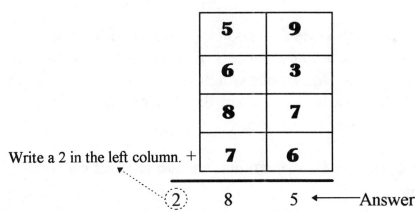

Write a 2 in the left column. +

2   8   5 ◄——Answer

Look at an example with three cards. The steps are the same as the previous example, except we are adding a place value.

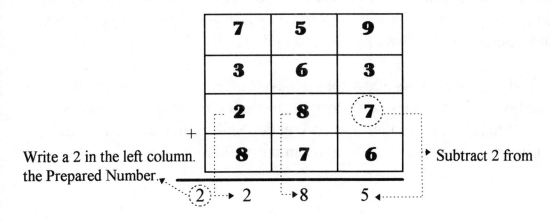

Write a 2 in the left column.
the Prepared Number.

Subtract 2 from

37

The sum 2 , 2 8 5 was obtained by following the three rules.

1) Subtract 2 from the Prepared Number.

2) Write the digits that are to the left of the Prepared Number.

3) Write a 2 in the left column.

Conclusion

Lightning Addition provides the classroom teacher with a new mathematics tool. It may be used by teachers of gifted students as well as in normal classroom situations. Best results will be achieved by explaining the routine in a series of small steps. Then, allow the students adequate time to analyze what has taken place.

Have the cards copied. If time permits, prepare separate cards for group investigation.

Many students will want to create their own Lightning Addition cards. Stress that there are many number combinations. Creative students might try and develop cards with sums in the thirties and forties. Key lines need not be the 2nd from the bottom but anywhere a student might choose.

Today's neon colors allow for the development of beautiful color combinations. They are aesthetically pleasing and capture the audience's attention. Student mathematics and art creation skills will be enhanced by using Lightning Addition in the classroom curriculum.

Use Lightning Addition to find the sums.

(1) 7	(2) 7	(3) 7	(4) 7
5	3	6	7
3	2	9	6
+ 6	+8	+5	+4
N	N	N	N

(5) 5 7	(6) 9 8	(7) 6 6	(8) 7 7	(9) 5 9
6 3	4 3	5 4	6 4	7 4
8 2	7 4	3 5	2 6	8 5
+7 8	+5 7	+7 8	+5 7	+6 5
N	N	N	N	N

(10) 7 5 7	(11) 5 7 7	(12) 8 7 9
7 6 6	6 5 3	3 5 4
6 8 9	8 3 2	4 3 7
+4 7 5	+7 6 8	+7 6 5
N	N	N

Answers:
1) 2 1	4) 2 4	7) 2 3 3	10) 2 6 8 7
2) 2 0	5) 2 8 0	8) 2 2 4	11) 2 8 3 0
3) 2 7	6) 2 7 2	9) 2 8 3	12) 2 4 3 5

LIGHTNING

WORKSHEET

A.

B.

C.

4	7	5	3
8	6	8	6
9	2	2	3
6	5	5	9
1	7	3	9
8	8	6	4
9	4	2	3
9	3	9	5

5	6	7	8
8	7	8	6
6	5	4	3
5	5	3	4
1	2	3	4
8	8	7	6
9	9	8	7
9	8	8	8

Create
your
own
card
magic.

The Impossible Paper

A simple geometric shape is displayed; yet, it seems nearly impossible to reproduce.

THE EFFECT

Students are instructed to observe a very unusual geometric configuration. A piece of paper has been cut, folded, and put on display for everyone to see, but not touch.

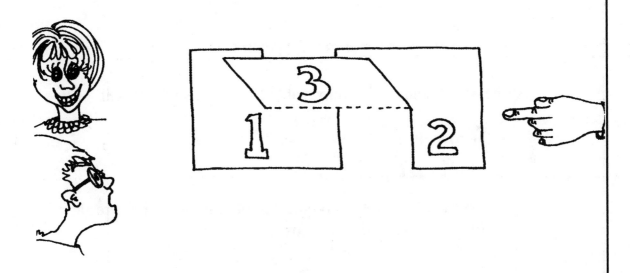

After a few minutes the class can be divided into groups. The groups are going to attempt to reproduce the observed paper.

Remove or cover the display. Distribute scissors and several sheets of 8 1/2 by 11 paper. Allow about 10 minutes for discussion and hands-on attempts to recreate the geometric project.

Junior and senior high school students are normally baffled by what appears to be a relatively simple task. Frequent comments might be "there is no possible solution; or, there is more than one sheet of paper." Reassure your students that there is a very simple, yet unorthodox, solution. And, there is just one sheet of paper.

As the mentor of the group you can help your students in two ways. First, you can guide the class to become alert observers. Second, you can demonstrate how to analyze a geometric problem from a seldom used but realistic and different perspective.

This paper challenge is called The Impossible Paper. The Impossible Paper uses a multifaceted approach to problem solving. Your class will gain enormous satisfaction when they have mastered the solution taken from the geometric science of topology.

OBJECTIVES

At the conclusion of The Impossible Paper the students will:

- Improve their participatory skills in group dynamics.

- Realize what appears to be a complex solution is the result of completing very simple steps.

- Understand the daily uses for some abstract geometric concepts.

- Discover how the science of mathematics is used to solve problems in architecture, engineering, and artistic design.

Preparation

Use a pencil and ruler to draw three lines on a rectangular piece of paper, creating three sections. See Illustration 1. Label the sections 1, 2, and 3.

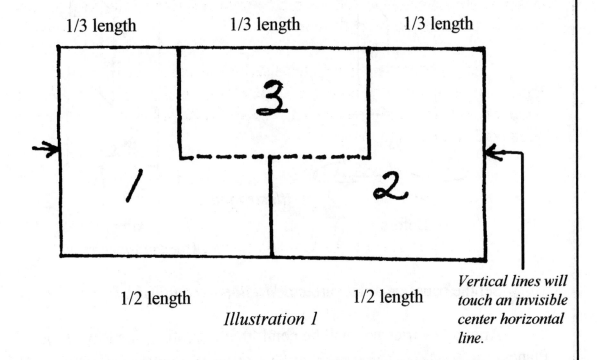

1/3 length   1/3 length   1/3 length

1/2 length   1/2 length

Vertical lines will touch an invisible center horizontal line.

Illustration 1

Draw a broken line across the bottom of section 3, an invisible center horizontal line. See Illustration 1.

Next, cut the solid lines that have just been drawn. The lines should be cut about 1/8" past the invisible center horizontal line. This will assist in folding the paper correctly.

The broken line is a fold line. Make a fine crease along its length. Be sure section 3 bends freely from front to back.

Hold the paper vertically with the left hand. Section 1 will now be at the top. With the right hand turn the bottom of the paper 180 degrees or a one-half rotation. See Illustration 2.

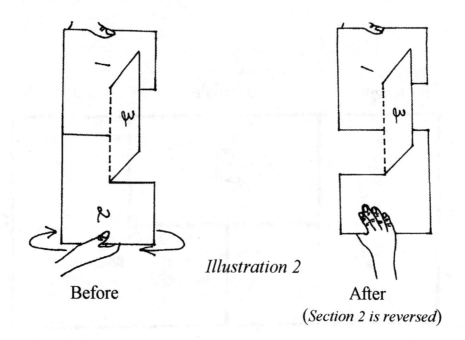

Illustration 2

Before

After

(*Section 2 is reversed*)

Set the paper on a flat surface. ***Mission accomplished***!

After a few tries you will be comfortable creating The Reversing Planes.

You will probably want to construct an Impossible Paper display using heavy poster board.

Laminate it. It stores easily and may be used for several years. Enjoy!

Conclusion

Students in grades 4 through 12 are always fascinated with this routine. As an educator, it will be especially pleasing to watch your students brainstorming. You may also guide them to create their own variations.

Have the class construct additional shapes by cutting and creasing the paper in a variety of directions. Cover some surfaces with aluminum foil, others with brightly colored fluorescent paper.

Punch a hole; tie a string. Suspend the design from a ceiling. The creative applications and uses for the exercise are numerous. Pleasing results can be achieved by students when they integrate science, mathematics, and artistic skills they have learned from The Impossible Paper.

Notes

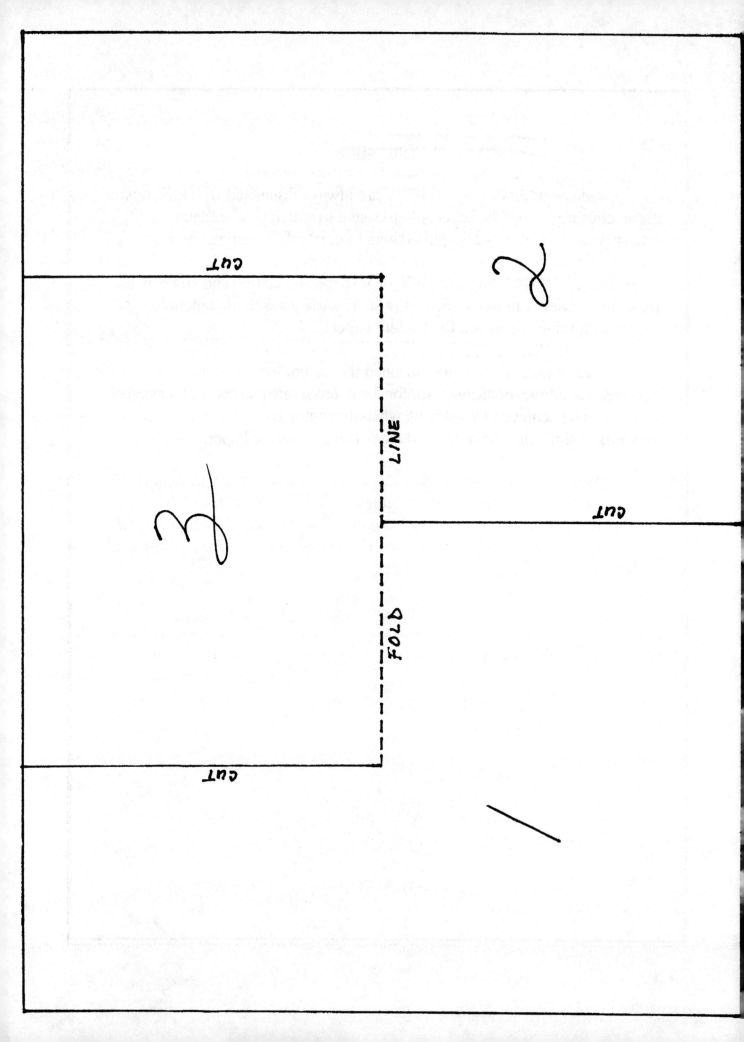

CUT

LINE

FOLD

CUT

CUT

2

3

1

The Jumping Paper Clips

Two separate paper clips are fastened to a piece of paper. Presto! They link together right before your eyes.

Effect

Show two paper clips, a rubber band, and a piece of paper about the size of a dollar. Fold the paper. Secure the fold with a paper clip. Put a rubber band on the paper. Place a second clip on the paper. Pull the ends of the paper slowly. Finish the pull with a sharp snap. The clips instantly jump onto the rubber band. The rubber band hangs freely from the paper.

Objectives

At the conclusion of The Jumping Paper Clips the students will:

- Have a greater understanding of the geometrical terms "surface" and "plane."

- Understand that solid objects can not pass through each other.

- Be able to demonstrate the physical characteristics of an open surface.

- Possess an understanding of the differences between open and closed paths.

<u>METHOD</u>

The success of the routine is dependent upon proper placement of the clips and the rubber band. Observers find it difficult to repeat the steps.

(1) Hold the paper open between both hands.

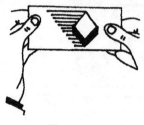
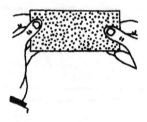

Front   *Back*

(2) With the front of the paper facing you, fold one-third the length of the paper to the right.

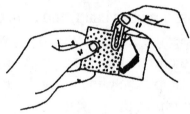

(3) Place one of the paper clips over the fold. Push the clip down so it is snug against the top of the paper. *Do not crease the paper. Just fold.*

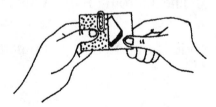

(4) Reverse the paper. Keep it right side up. The first clip will still be at the top. Place a rubber band around the paper from the left. Be sure the rubber band does not go past the paper clip.

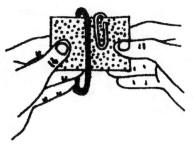

(5) Fold the left-hand side of the paper to the right. The left end should be near the right edge of the paper. *Again, do not crease the paper.* The paper is now divided into three equal segments.

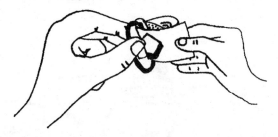

(6) **Note, the proper placement of the second paper clip is an integral part of the routine. Care should be taken.** In the above illustration, notice there are two loops in the paper. The second paper clip is placed half way inside the loop closest to your right hand. Insert the clip with one-half to the outside front and the other half inside the loop. When both clips have been properly placed, the folded paper will look like the illustration below.

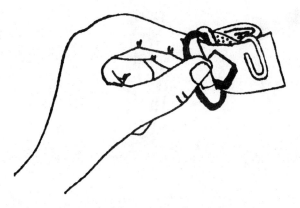

(7) Tightly grasp both ends of the paper near the top. At first pull slowly. When the paper unfolds, the clips will start moving together. They are still pinned to the paper. When the clips are close to each other, give the paper a sharp tug.

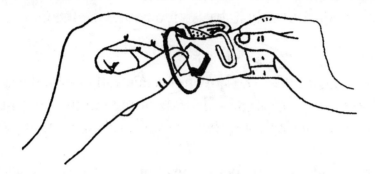

(9) The paper will open. The paper clips jump onto the rubber band. The band hangs from the paper. They can be examined by all and shown to be linked together.

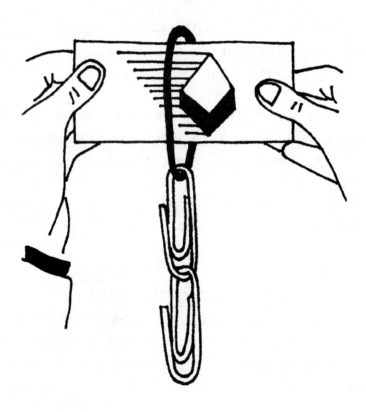

Conclusion

My students have all shown a keen interest in the Linking Paper Clips. They gain a lot of satisfaction when they demonstrate the technique to friends.

Once the students understand how to successfully make the paper clips link, be sure and stress the topological aspects of the routine. Important mathematical concepts will be lost if they are not explained during the demonstration.

The two clips share a common plane. As the paper is pulled, the clips advance to the center of the paper. When the center is reached, the two clips interlock. This forces the clips to move in a vertical direction and off the paper.

Jumping off the paper is exactly what would happen if it were not for the rubber band. The three objects share a common plane with the paper. The clips have an open plane. This allows them to cross one another and join together.

The rubber band is a closed plane. When the open and closed planes meet, they interlock. The clips can not jump; they simply dangle from the rubber band.

COMMENTS AND SUGGESTIONS

Today paper clips come in a variety of colors. They come in large sizes and can be purchased at an office supply store. Try jumbo paper clips. They are long and wide. The linking can be followed very easily.

Notes

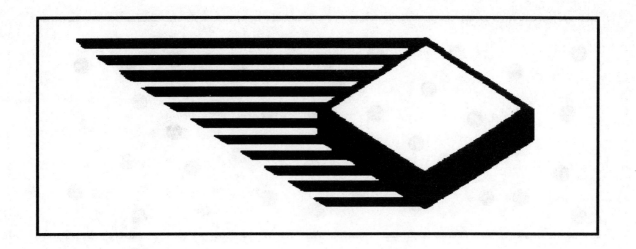

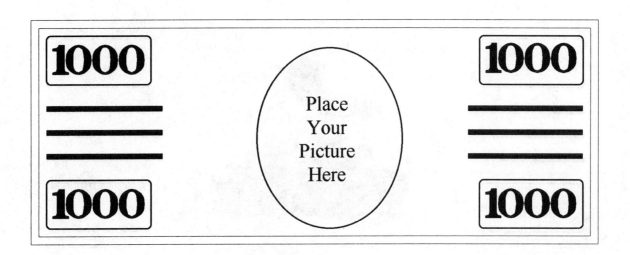

Design your own.

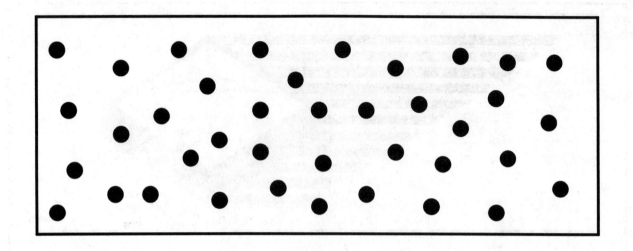

Design your own.

THE STRING ESCAPE

Students are loosely bound together at the wrists. It appears impossible to release them without cutting or untying the yarn. A clever topological manipulation solves the problem.

The Effect

Two students are connected with long pieces of yarn. Their task is to separate themselves. No untying or cutting is allowed.

Yes, it is possible!

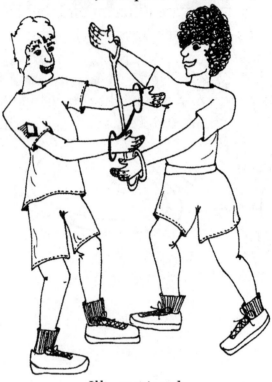

Illustration 1

Objectives

After completing The String Escape, your students will:

- Have a better understanding of the terms topology and geometry.

- See a relationship between certain mathematical terms and real life objects.

- Become better at understanding and following directions.

- Realize the advantages of cooperation, team work, and learning through participation.

Preparation

This activity is a great for the classroom. It takes minimal preparation time. When it's over, there's no mess.

The only materials needed are different different colored rolls of yarn. The yarn should by cut in 45-55 inch lengths. The length will depend on the size and age of your students.

Divide the class into partners. Each partner should have a different colored string. Today we will use two colors, blue and white.

Follow these steps:

1) The person with the blue string is to tie one end to a wrist. When completed, tie the second end to the other wrist. Both wrists are now bound by yarn. For younger students, this activity can be tricky. Remind the students to work as a team and help the other person, if needed.

2) Instruct the student with the white string to tie only **one** end to a wrist.

3) Next, have the partners face each other. The person with the blue string should hold his/her arms in a horizontal position. The person with the white yarn is to hold the right arm in the air, above the head.

4) The student with the white string can take the free end and place it behind their partner's yarn. The free end can now be tied to the free wrist.

5) The students should now appear like the figures in Illustration 1.

The students are to separate themselves. They may not cut, untie, or break the string. The yarn is to stay around the wrists at all times. Finally, they may only use their bodies.

Before you explain the solution, let them have an opportunity to explore the many possibilities. Let them work for a couple of days. Take pieces home to work with parents. This is a great way to challenge your whole class.

The Method

The solution is relatively simple. Follow steps 1 through 5.

1) Both participants face one another. They should be in their original positions. The blue is horizontal. The white is vertical.

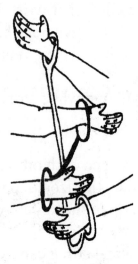

2) The strings are now perpendicular. To solve the problem the strings must slide past each other. The white string will move to the right wrist of the person holding the blue string.

3) The student with the white string will use his/her **left** hand and reach through the loop. Using their fingers, grasp the white yarn. Pull it through the blue loop. Be sure and bring it above the partner's wrist and fingers.

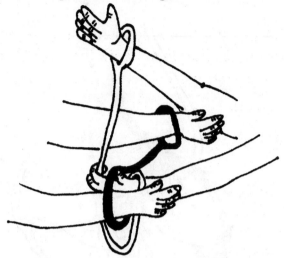

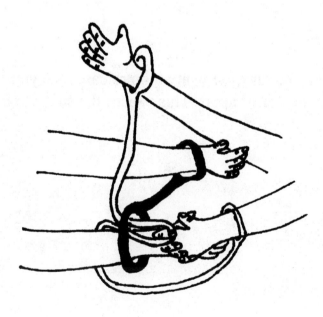

4) Be careful with the final steps. Bring the white yarn underneath the partners finger tips and wrists.

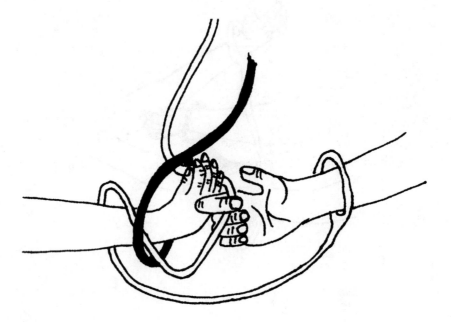

5) The person holding the white loop releases the yarn. Very slowly, each partner pulls their arms apart. This causes the string to become separate.

Conclusion

The Releasing Bracelet is an outstanding way to introduce topology[1] to your class. All will have a great time exploring and investigating. Surprises may abound. Students will admit they never thought math would be so much fun!

You may want to use more than a class period for this activity. If time is a factor, as little as twenty minutes can be used to work on the solution. The explanation lasts about five minutes.

That's it.

Spend twenty-five minutes and some might be excited enough to want to know more about additional fun things in geometry. If this occurs send them to the library and bring back information on the Mobius (Möe'-bi-us) Strip.[2]

[1]Topology is a branch of geometry that studies the configuration of shapes.

[2] Named after August Mobius. The strip is actually a geometric construction that seems to have two surfaces; but, it is really just one long continuous surface. Construction requires a long strip of paper. One end is held stationary. The other is rotated one half turn, 180 degrees. Both ends are glued.

Notes

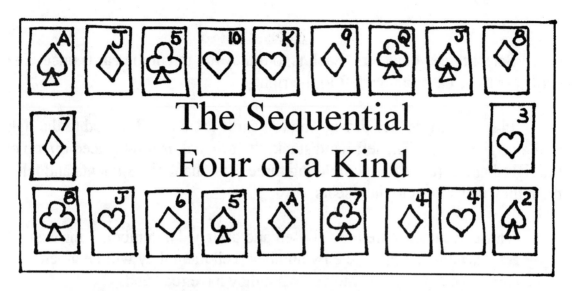

Cards are shuffled and dealt. All players think they have a great hand. But....

THE EFFECT

Display a standard deck of playing cards, 52 in all. Make sure the jokers have been removed. The cards are arranged in suits from ace through king. One might get the impression the cards have never been shuffled, just like a new deck. Fan and display the cards for all to see.

Select three volunteers. Each is told they are to cut the cards once. The cards are to be cut from the left to the right.

Place the cards face down. The top cards are cut and placed to the right of the original stack. The left-hand stack, the original, is now placed on top of the right-hand cards. After completing three cuts, thank the students and tell them they may return to their seats.

Thirteen students are now chosen and assigned a number, 1 through 13. They are placed in a large circle by number. Tell them they will be given some cards, but may not look to see what they have received.

Slowly count as the cards are dealt 1, 2, 3, ... 12, 13. When the thirteenth card has been dealt, return to number one and repeat the process. Continue until all 52 cards are distributed. Each student receives 4 cards.

Next, ask the students if they are familiar with the game of poker and if they know what makes a good hand. Nearly all will respond in the affirmative.

Tell the students they may look at their cards. Do not show or tell anyone what they are holding.

Ask someone, "Would you be satisfied if you held these four cards in a card game?"

The answer is always a definite, "Yes!"

On the count of three, the students may turn over their cards for all to see. The result is each person holds four of a kind. The cards are also sequential 7, 8 , 9 etc.

Your students will improve their understanding of mathematical patterning after they have learned the secret of the math magic routine known as The Sequential Four of a Kind.

The Objectives

After the students have mastered The Sequential Four of a Kind, the following objectives should be achieved:

- There will be an increased awareness that what appears to be chaos might actually be highly organized patterning.

- An insight into mathematical patterning will be gained.

- The students will be exposed to some basic concepts of game theory.

- The class will have improved their abilities to predict an outcome based on limited information.

Preparation

The Sequential Four of a Kind is an example of what occurs when there is a fixed and recurring pattern. In the fixed and recurring pattern, once a sequence has been established it continues indefinitely.

This unusual demonstration is self-working. Follow these steps:

1) Remove the jokers from a standard card deck. Arrange the cards by suits. Order them from ace through king. Alternate the suits black, red, black, red.

2) Place the cards on a flat surface and select volunteers to cut the deck. The cards are to be cut from left to right. After the cut, pick up the left pile and place it on top of the right pile. The deck may be cut as many times as you like. A maximum of three cuts is recommended. If additional cuts are made, have no fear. The result will not change.

3) Explain that thirteen student volunteers will be needed. Tell the students they will be given some cards to hold. They should not look at them nor may they mix them up. If the room is large, arrange the students in a circular pattern.

4) Deal out the cards one at a time. As the cards are distributed count one, two, three....eleven, twelve, thirteen. When thirteen is reached, start again with one. Continue the counting and distribution until all the cards are handed to the students. Each student will have four cards.

5) Ask the students if they are familiar with the game of poker. Most will respond in the affirmative. Now explain that the card holders may take a quick glance at their hands. Look at the cards but do not allow anyone else to see. When this has been done, inquire if they are satisfied with their cards. Again, the response will be affirmative.

6) Announce you are going to count to three. On three the cards are to be turned over and displayed for all to see.

ONE

TWO

THREE

When everyone has the chance to see the effect, they will be impressed.

Three observations can be made. (1) Everyone holds four of a kind. (2) The cards are sequential, ace through king. (3) The suits follow a set pattern.[1]

[1]Occasionally, a student will mix the cards while holding them. Caution about mixing the cards. If the pattern is broken there is no need to mention it. Everyone will still enjoy seeing the four of a kind and the sequencing.

Why It Works

When the cards are cut, a mental illusion takes place. Our minds are conditioned to think the arrangement of the cards has changed. In reality, there is no mixing at any time. The pattern, ace through king, and the arrangement of the suits is unchanged.

Reviewing the steps reveals that the cards are cut from the pile and placed on the right. The teacher then places the uncut portion, now on the left, back on the right pile. This step is integral to understanding the effect. By moving the cards from left to right the pattern remains unbroken. The positioning of the cards in the deck has changed, but the pattern remains fixed and recurring.

Cutting and shuffling of cards are two entirely different processes. Had the deck been shuffled, the arrangement of the cards would have been altered. The outcome would have been completely modified; there would have been no magic.

Finally, the routine works because of the characteristics of a standard card deck. The deck has 52 cards consisting of 4 suits. Each suit has 13 different cards.

It will be recalled that 13 volunteers were selected to be card holders, the exact number of cards in a suit. Imagine that the first student was given a three of spades. Thirteen cards later the teacher would return and deal another card. This card would be a red three, either diamonds or hearts. The volunteer will receive two more threes; there are now four threes being held by the unsuspecting student. It all happens because the cards are never shuffled.

REMEMBER: ALL THE CARDS ONLY CHANGE POSITION IN THE DECK WHEN CUTTING TAKE PLACE . THE INTERNAL POSITION OF THE CARDS REMAINS THE SAME WHEN A FIXED AND REPEATING PATTERN HAS BEEN ESTABLISHED.

CONCLUSION

The Sequential Four of a Kind requires no sleight-of-hand. When the steps are mastered it becomes self-working magic. Chances are, the students will give you their undivided attention when they are taught how to perform the routine.

They will surely be surprised to find the solution involves several simple and non-complicated steps.

Notes

Social Security Number Test

Teach the art of memorization. Use an unusual mathematics' principle to memorize 30 social security numbers.....All in five minutes!

The Effect

The teacher asks, "How many of you have your social security number memorized?"

Some of the students will raise their hand. Next, ask if anyone could tell their parent's social security number. The class may have lots of trouble with this. The teacher then says she has memorized 30 social security numbers of friends and relatives.

As the class professes their disbelief, the teacher produces a deck of 30 cards. They are distributed and freely investigated by all. On the front side is a number, and a person's name. On the reverse side is a social security number.

After the investigation the cards are collected and handed to someone in the classroom. They may be shuffled. A card is selected, any card. The person's name and number are read.

After a few moments the teacher proceeds to write a social security number on the classroom chalkboard. The volunteer holding the card is asked to read the number. Amazingly, the numbers match.

Objectives

At the conclusion of the Social Security Test your students will:

- Learn to use number-reversal patterns.

- Have an understanding of how to cast out numbers.

- Be able to use the addition of numbers in horizontal rows to predict an outcome.

- Gain a new tool in fact memorization.

The Method

On the front of each card is a number, 1 through 30, and a person's name. On the reverse is a nine-digit number.

Surprisingly, the magician does not know the social security number. It can be deduced by following a number development pattern.

The initial step is to listen for the number on the identification card. Maybe the volunteer read the following:

" Number 17......... Mike Hesse "

or

" Number 30.........Carmen D. Wilson"

The name on the card is not important .... rather, it is the number that accompanies the name.

Mike Hesse's social security number is 921-34-7189.
The number 17 holds the key to the nine-digit number. Likewise, Carmen D. Wilson's 30 allowed the teacher to write the number 246-06-6280.

Step 1)   To deduce the number follow these steps.
First, mentally add 12 to the number supplied.

$$17 + 12 = 29$$
and
$$30 + 12 = 42$$

Step 2)   Second, reverse the new number.

The reversal of 29 is 92.
and
The reversal of 42 is 24

Step 3) Add all digits horizontally. <u>Cast out all ones digits in the tens place.</u>

Fill in the spaces on Mike Hesse's social security card.

9 2 __ - __ __ - __ __ __ __

$9 + 2 = 1\,1$ REMEMBER to cast out the one in the tens place. So, $9 + 2 = 1$.

9 2 1 - __ __ - __ __ __ __

$2 + 1 = 3$

9 2 1 - 3 __ - __ __ __ __

$1 + 3 = 4$

9 2 1 - 3 4 - __ __ __ __

$3 + 4 = 7$

9 2 1 - 3 4 - 7 __ __ __

$4 + 7 = 1$ REMEMBER, cast out the 1 in the tens place.

9 2 1 - 3 4 - 7 1 __ __

$7 + 1 = 8$

9 2 1 - 3 4 - 7 1 8 __

$1 + 8 = 9$

9 2 1 - 3 4 - 7 1 8 9

Fill in the missing digits.

Name	Card number	Add 12	Reversal	First 5 digits
Mike Hesse	17	29	92	9 2 1 - 3 4
Jay Roberts	31	43	A	3 4 7 - 1 8
Sharon Lehan	3	1B	51	5C 6 - 7 3
Jerry Thomas	6	D	E 1	8 F 9- 09
Terry Waldron	27	G	H	I 3 2- J K

A)_____   B)_____   C)_____   D)_____   E)_____   F)_____

G)_____   H)_____   I)_____   J)_____   K)_____

Answers: A) 34, B) 5, C) 1, D) 18, E) 8, F) 1,
G) 39, H) 93, I) 9, J) 5, K) 7

Fill in the social security number

Number	Name	social security number
9	Brian Fox	1 2 __ - __ __ - __ __ __ __
11	Elda Volner	3 __ 5 - __ __ - __ __ 0 __
15	Jonathan Pautler	7__ __ - __ __ - 1 __ __ __
19	Wanda Hupp	__ __ __ - 7 1 - __ __ __ __
26	Jamie Hartmann	__ __ __ - __ __ - __ __ __ __
29	Clarence Kinzel	__ __ __ - __ __ - __ __ __ __

Refer to the cards at the end of this chapter for the correct answers.

Conclusion

When we first started the investigation of our social security routine, it seemed there was no relationship between the numbers on the cards, front or back. The fact is all the numbers are closely related. There is a definite pattern.

Study these examples in sequential patterning:

#	Name	Social Security Number
1	Albert Engfield	314-59-4370
2	Walter Belson	415-61-7853
3	Sharon Lehan	516-73-0336
4	Dana Stamm	617-85-3819
5	Cindy Clark	718-97-6392
6	Jerry Thomas	819-09-9875
7	Pat Junk	910-11-2358

By looking at cards 1 through 7 several interesting things are revealed. (1) All the first and third numbers are sequential 3, 4, 5.... (2) The second numbers are all 1's.

A quick glance at the list of names and numbers shows a definite patterning sequence throughout the number column, 1 through 7.

Before showing the list to the students, it would be wise to spend a few moments reviewing the concept of casting out digits and horizontal addition.

There are many ways your students can create their own pattern cards. Think about it. Try it on telephone numbers, employee identification cards, or even household appliances.

Allow students adequate time to develop their ideas. You might be surprised at the student generated uses for the mathematical concepts of number reversals, casting out digits, and horizontal addition.

1
Albert Engfield

2
Walter Belson

3
Sharon Lehan

4
Dana Stamm

5
Cindy Clark

314-59-4370

415-61-7853

516-73-0336

617-85-3819

718-97-6392

6

Jerry Thomas

7

Pat Junk

8

Jack Markley

9

Brian Fox

10

Mike Sparks

819-09-9875

910-11-2358

022-46-0662

123-58-3145

224-60-6628

11
Elda Volner

12
Paul Nicholson

13
Edith Mathis

14
Erin Shannon

15
Jonathan Pautler

325-72-9101

426-84-2684

527-96-5167

628-08-8640

729-10-1123

16
Pat Bauman

17
Mike Hesse

18
Lynn Hughes

19
Wanda Hupp

20
Andrew Belsky

820-22-4606

921-34-7189

033-69-5493

134-71-8976

235-83-1459

21
Edna Laufer

22
John Beckerson

23
Susan Walkup

24
Kathy Anderson

25
Carol Riley

336-95-4932

437-07-7415

538-19-0998

639-21-3471

730-33-6954

26
Jamie Hartmann

27
Terry Waldron

28
Rita Tendick

29
Clarence Kinzel

30
Carmen D. Wilson

831-45-9437

932-57-2910

044-82-0224

145-94-3707

246-06-6280

Use these blank boxes to put in a friends name.

31

_____

32

_____

33

_____

34

_____

Continue the pattern.

**Remember to use the numbers
on the front sheet.**

_____ - _____ - _____

_____ - _____ - _____

_____ - _____ - _____

_____ - _____ - _____

Dear Teacher,
I would like to tell you about two magic routines. If you like them, could I show the class?
This is my description:

Interview the next magician to visit your school. In the space provided list four questions you might ask. Be sure and leave an answer space between the questions. A box is located to the right of the interview sheet. Use it to draw a picture of a magic routine.

PRISM DAILY SPEAKER

EARLY EDITION................EVERYDAY....

THE THINGS I LIKE MOST ABOUT MAGIC ARE.....

1) _____

_____

_____

2) _____

_____

_____

3) _____

_____

_____

4) _____

_____

_____

5) _____

_____

_____